COOL CARS

MASERATI

BY DALTON RAINS

WWW.APEXEDITIONS.COM

Copyright © 2026 by Apex Editions, Mendota Heights, MN 55120. All rights reserved. No part of this book may be reproduced or utilized in any form or by any means without written permission from the publisher.

Apex is distributed by North Star Editions:
sales@northstareditions.com | 888-417-0195

Produced for Apex by Red Line Editorial.

Photographs ©: Pexels, cover; Shutterstock Images, 1, 6–7, 9, 13, 15, 18–19, 20–21, 24–25, 26–27, 29; Pbpgalleries/Alamy, 4–5; Neil/Flickr, 8; Klemantaski Collection/Hulton Archive/Getty Images, 10–11; iStockphoto, 12, 14; John Keeble/Getty Images News/Getty Images, 16–17; Cristian Cristel/Xinhua News Agency/Newscom, 22–23

Library of Congress Control Number: 2025930305

ISBN
979-8-89250-523-9 (hardcover)
979-8-89250-559-8 (paperback)
979-8-89250-630-4 (ebook pdf)
979-8-89250-595-6 (hosted ebook)

Printed in the United States of America
Mankato, MN
082025

NOTE TO PARENTS AND EDUCATORS

Apex books are designed to build literacy skills in striving readers. Exciting, high-interest content attracts and holds readers' attention. The text is carefully leveled to allow students to achieve success quickly. Additional features, such as bolded glossary words for difficult terms, help build comprehension.

CHAPTER 1
ROAD TRIP 4

CHAPTER 2
HISTORY 10

CHAPTER 3
MODERN MASERATIS 16

CHAPTER 4
OTHER OPTIONS 22

COMPREHENSION QUESTIONS • 28
GLOSSARY • 30
TO LEARN MORE • 31
ABOUT THE AUTHOR • 31
INDEX • 32

CHAPTER 1

ROAD TRIP

A driver speeds through mountain roads. The engine of her Maserati GranCabrio roars. All-wheel drive helps the car zoom up steep slopes.

A Maserati GranCabrio can hit 60 miles per hour (97 km/h) in 3.6 seconds.

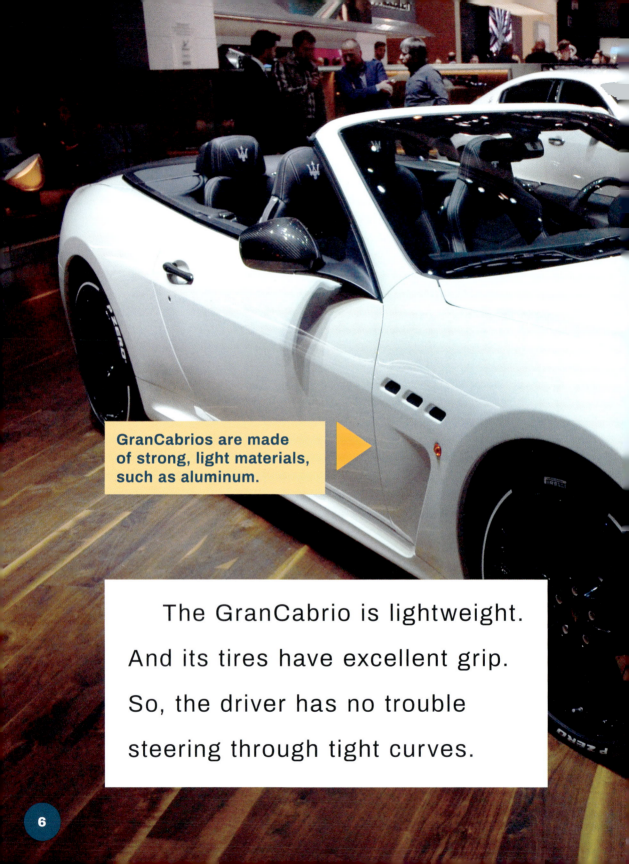

GranCabrios are made of strong, light materials, such as aluminum.

The GranCabrio is lightweight. And its tires have excellent grip. So, the driver has no trouble steering through tight curves.

FAST FACT

GranCabrios can go 180 miles per hour (290 km/h).

GranCabrio seats have neck warmers. That way, drivers stay comfortable while the top is down.

Soon, the car coasts down a hill. The driver presses a button. The roof folds down. Now, she can feel the wind. She loves exploring the world in her GranCabrio.

GRAND TOURERS

The GranCabrio is a grand tourer (GT). GTs are made to drive long distances at high speeds. The cars are comfortable and roomy. They also have powerful engines.

The GranCabrio has four driving modes. One is GT mode. One is for comfort. Others are for speed.

CHAPTER 2

History

Three brothers started Maserati in 1914. The company built its first race car in 1926. Soon, Maseratis were winning races.

A Maserati speeds along the track during a 1938 race.

After World War II (1939–1945), Maserati started making sports cars and GTs. The A6 1500 Gran Turismo came out in 1947. This **coupe** was Maserati's first road-legal car.

Gran turismo means "grand touring" in Italian.

The first Maserati Quattroporte had a top speed of 143 miles per hour (230 km/h).

LONG-LIVED LINES

The first Quattroporte came out in 1963. It was the fastest **sedan** of the 1960s. In 1966, the sporty Ghibli first arrived. These lines became popular for decades.

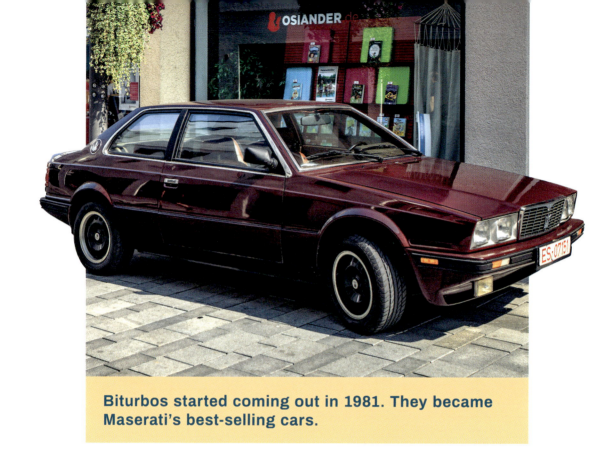

Biturbos started coming out in 1981. They became Maserati's best-selling cars.

The sharp-edged Maserati Bora hit the road in the 1970s. Less-expensive Biturbo models arrived in the 1980s. Maserati had become a top carmaker.

FAST FACT
In 2004, the MC12 became Maserati's fastest road-legal car. It could rocket past 205 miles per hour (330 km/h).

Maserati built just 50 MC12s.

CHAPTER 3

MODERN MASERATIS

Maserati continued to make beautiful, speedy cars. GranTurismos had classic Maserati curves, vents, and grilles. But LED lights gave the cars a modern touch.

In 1926, Maserati began using a logo shaped like a trident. This shape still appears on Maserati grilles.

Maserati began selling MC20s in 2020. Their engines were based on Maserati's **Formula 1** race cars. Like race cars, MC20s turned and **accelerated** quickly. But they were still comfortable inside.

MANY MC20s

Maserati made several versions of the MC20. Cielos were **convertibles**. Nottes were painted black. Leggendas were mint-green and black. It used the colors of a winning race car in the 2000s.

The MC20 featured sporty butterfly doors.

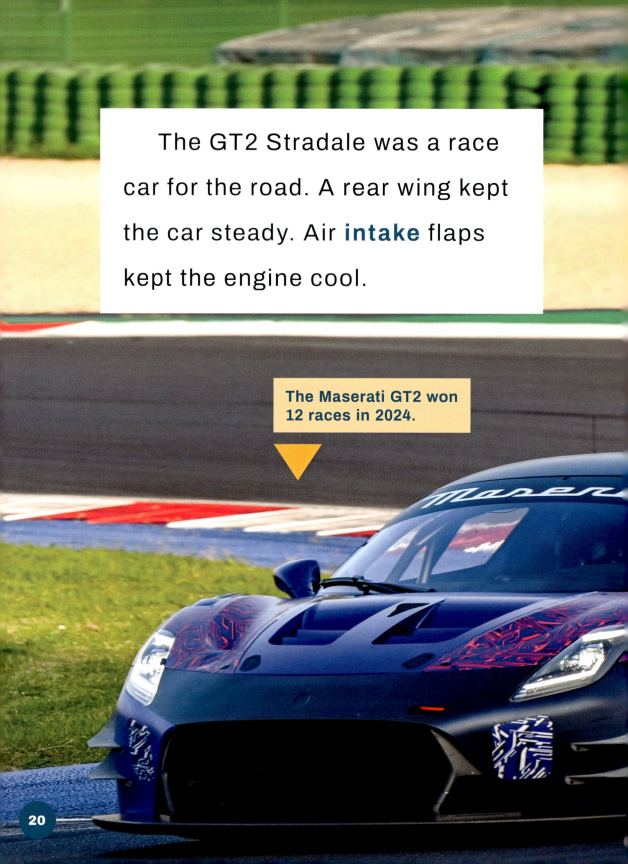

The GT2 Stradale was a race car for the road. A rear wing kept the car steady. Air **intake** flaps kept the engine cool.

The Maserati GT2 won 12 races in 2024.

FAST FACT

GT2 Stradales could reach 60 miles per hour (97 km/h) in 2.8 seconds.

CHAPTER 4

OTHER OPTIONS

In the 2020s, Maserati began moving away from gasoline engines. People could buy electric GranCabrios, GranTurismos, and more. These models were called Folgores.

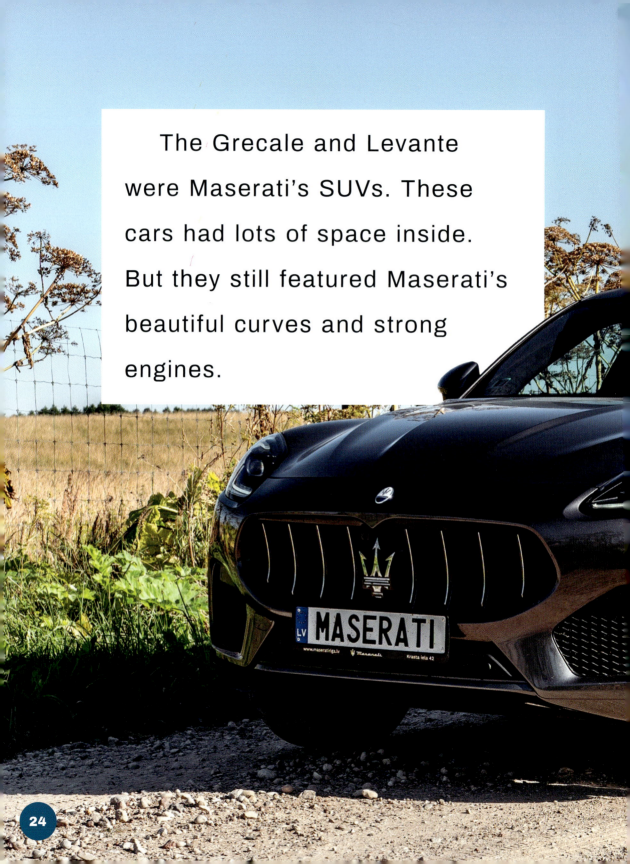

The Grecale and Levante were Maserati's SUVs. These cars had lots of space inside. But they still featured Maserati's beautiful curves and strong engines.

FAST FACT
The Levante had improved **suspension** for rough, off-road driving.

Maserati SUVs had all-wheel drive.

MCXtrema

The MCXtrema was a track-only car. Parts of its **design** were based on race cars from the 1960s. It had a low body and sharp, sporty fins.

Maserati made only 62 MCXtremas.

Maserati built rare cars, too. The Ghibli 334 Ultima was a superfast sedan. The F Tributo Special Edition honored the first female Formula 1 driver. Fans couldn't wait for what Maserati would put on the road next.

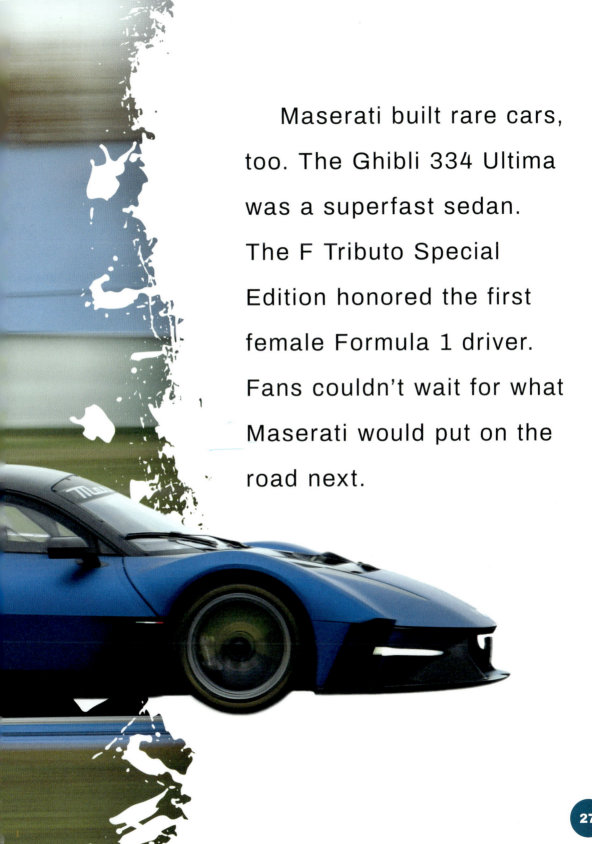

COMPREHENSION
QUESTIONS

Write your answers on a separate piece of paper.

1. Write a few sentences explaining the main ideas of Chapter 2.

2. Which Maserati model would you most like to have? Why?

3. When was Maserati's first race car built?
   - A. 1914
   - B. 1926
   - C. 1947

4. How many years after the release of the first Quattroporte did the first Ghibli arrive?
   - A. two years
   - B. three years
   - C. four years

5. What does **classic** mean in this book?

*GranTurismos had **classic** Maserati curves, vents, and grilles. But LED lights gave the cars a modern touch.*

    A. based on the past
    B. happening in the future
    C. not used in real life

6. What does **versions** mean in this book?

*Maserati made several **versions** of the MC20. Cielos were convertibles. Nottes were painted black.*

    A. models that are not sold
    B. models that are the exact same
    C. models that have small differences

Answer key on page 32.

GLOSSARY

accelerated
Sped up.

convertibles
Cars with tops that can come down or be taken off.

coupe
A type of car that is usually smaller and sportier than a sedan.

design
The way something looks or is made.

Formula 1
The highest level of open-wheel racing.

intake
A part that lets something in.

sedan
A car that seats at least four people comfortably.

suspension
A system of parts that supports a vehicle and helps handle bumps and dips in the road.

BOOKS

Duling, Kaitlyn. *Maserati MC20*. Bellwether Media, 2024.

Hamilton, S. L. *Maserati*. Abdo Publishing, 2023.

Peterson, Megan Cooley. *Maserati GranTurismo*. Black Rabbit Books, 2021.

ONLINE RESOURCES

Visit **www.apexeditions.com** to find links and resources related to this title.

ABOUT THE AUTHOR

Dalton Rains is a writer and editor from St. Paul, Minnesota. He would love to drive a Maserati someday.

INDEX

A
A6 1500 Gran Turismo, 12

B
Biturbo, 14
Bora, 14

F
F Tributo Special Edition, 27
Folgores, 22
Formula 1, 18, 27

G
Ghibli, 13
Ghibli 334 Ultima, 27
GranCabrio, 4, 6–9, 22
GranTurismos, 16, 22
Grecale, 24
GT2 Stradale, 20–21

L
Levante, 24–25

M
MC12, 15
MC20, 18
MCXtrema, 26

Q
Quattroporte, 13

W
World War II, 12

ANSWER KEY:
1. Answers will vary; 2. Answers will vary; 3. B; 4. B; 5. A; 6. C